Green Smoothie Recipes For Weight Loss

The Healthy Green Smoothie Recipes To Cleanse, Detox And Lose Weight

Russell Warren

DISCLAIMER

The ideas, procedures, and suggestions in this book are intended as a source of information and not as substitute for treatment by or medical advices of a professional health care provider.The author have endeavored to ensure that the information presented is accurate and up to date. However, your should consult your doctor or health care provider before adopting the suggestions in this book, as well as about any condition that may require diagnosis or medical attention. The author and publisher disclaim any liability arising directly or indirectly from the use of the book.

CONTENTS

INTRODUCTION

Losing weight can be a struggle, especially if you feel like you are caught up in a cycle of following one fad diet after another. Many fad diets leave you feeling unsatisfied or hungry, and both feelings may decrease your likelihood of sticking to the diet. What if there was a way to maintain your current eating habits, making only slight changes to your diet, while still losing weight? This isn't some miracle drug or another fad diet; it is a "Green Smoothie Recipes" plan.

The book Green Smoothie Recipes : 'Green Smoothie Recipes For Weight Loss : The Healthy Green Smoothie Recipes To Cleanse, Detox And Lose Weight " is a collection of green smoothie recipes for those who hunt for an effective weight loss plan that doesn't put a strain on their health. It is a big companion for dieters who crave to lose a few inches & pounds while enjoying their ride to a healthy body. These Green smoothies drinks contain fresh fruit & leafy greens such as spinach, arugula or kale. Green smoothies are vital source of amino acids. Fruit makes these green smoothies delicious. Greens make these smoothies nutritional powerhouses. Leafy greens are included among the super foods & are rich in vitamins A and C, calcium, magnesium, potassium and iron. These green smoothie drinks contain omega-3 unsaturated fat, which are beneficial to a healthy immune system. Greens can be combined with any other food & enhance digestion by stimulating enzyme production

The weight loss properties of green smoothies are healthful and also make them useful. Nutrition Experts recommend these green smoothies because these provide so many nutrients in a single glass serving that you lose the desire to overeat & to eat foods that lead to weight gain. As your body obtains the nutrition it needs & desires, the pounds start to melt away without the drama of fad diets. Don't think of green smoothie recipes as a quick fix for weight loss. Think of them as a part of new & healthy lifestyle from which you reap nutritional benefits, including weight loss. Whatever your goals, whether it's your quest for vibrant health, weight loss or shape management, incorporating green smoothies will be the exposure you have been looking for! Welcome to "Green Smoothie Recipes" Magic.

The book Green Smoothie Recipes : 'Green Smoothie Recipes For Weight Loss : The Healthy Green Smoothie Recipes To Cleanse, Detox And Lose Weight " is ideal for those who want to begin on a juicy diet & even for those who are already juicing for weight loss & want to keep it healthy all the way.

CHAPTER 1 - WHAT IS GREEN SMOOTHIE?

A green smoothie is a blend of various fruits and green vegetables like watermelon, lemon, spinach, cucumbers, and celery. The fundamental idea behind this is to provide all the health benefits at one go. Green smoothie has great taste and includes all the nutrients of delicious fruits and leafy vegetables.The green smoothies are very helpful for those individuals who don't take the recommended amount of nutrients in their daily diet. According to some studies conducted in USA it is estimated that one third of children don't even consume two cups of fruits and vegetables daily. This makes them deficient in proteins and nutrients.

If anyone asks you about your intake of green leafy vegetables in your diet then what will be your answer? Not a lot of them may be. In fact people not even have the green vegetables in salads also. The salad which is prepared is loaded with lots of fats and sugars which don't serve any purpose in our diet. It is better to consume it raw, rather than with cream or salt or sugar. So it is suggested to go for green smoothies.It is a good choice to add vegetables to the fruit based smoothie. This is considered to be a very healthy choice these day. There is so much that we can get from these vegetables and fruits. They are rich source of minerals, vitamin A and C, fiber, proteins etc. It is always advised to include the green vegetables while blending the fruits for making smoothies.

Green Smoothies can be prepared in seconds. It can be called as the fast food by nature. People have started adding this in their daily diet. They are even inculcating this habit in their children. It is suggested to consume the green smoothie immediately after making it. This is because if we will keep the smoothie for long time then all its nutrients will be lost.

CHAPTER 2 - WHY GREEN SMOOTHIE IS A BETTER CHOICE THAN OTHER SMOOTHIES?

It is always suggested to go for green smoothie rather than normal fruit smoothies. It is considered to be the most incredible drink that we should add in our daily diet. It is a perfect way to keep a check on all the nutrients, vitamins and fiber content in our body. It is the best way to overcome yours as well as your family's health problems. Including smoothies in the diet is very helpful. There are people who neglect the green leafy vegetables in their diet. This is very wrong. They are unaware of the importance of green leafy vegetables in the diet. The green leafy vegetables have high chlorophyll content which is very beneficial for gaining energy. The smoothies with green vegetables in them also help in nourishing our body.

Green smoothies are also a very good source of providing fiber to our body. Lack of fiber content in the body often leads to toxins. So it is better to include a glass of green smoothie in your daily diet. Green smoothie is also a very good nutrient diet for the kids. The kids are often prone to health diseases as their immune system is not fully developed. So it is advised to give them a diet which is rich in all the nutrients and vitamins.

Moreover green smoothies are very delicious in taste. The kids will enjoy it. Inspite of having the cold drinks and other aerated drinks they should be given these drinks in their diet. It is the best way to eat delicious fruits and vegetables daily. There are so many other health benefits of consuming green smoothie daily. Some of them are:-

- Increases our body energy
- Helps in reducing weight
- Prevents from chronic sickness
- Faster recovery of injuries

It is also considered as the best way for people who are not able to eat the raw vegetables. By mixing the green vegetables with fruits they can easily drink it. Moreover it is very easy to digest. According to a survey it is showed that chewing leads to forty percent of the absorption of food while blending leads to ninety percent of the digestion. So it is very clear that drinking a glass of smoothie is far better than having a bowl of salad daily.

CHAPTER 3 - WHAT IS THE NUTRITIONAL CONTENT OF GREEN SMOOTHIES?

Today the individuals have become more health conscious. They are aware of the health benefits. They exercise, take drug therapies, consult dietitians and take a diet rich in vitamin B complex, minerals and antioxidants. People who don't have time for workout and don't prefer going to a dietitian can opt for a simple way to keep healthy and i.e. by including the green smoothies in their daily diet. The green smoothies provide many nutritional benefits to an individual.

Green smoothie is a good source of minerals, iron, proteins, copper, vitamin B1, B2, B6, niacin, folate, carbohydrates etc. The fruits and vegetables can be used in combination to have all the nutrients in our diet. All these fruits and vegetables have different nutritional content which can be taken in combined form. Of late the green smoothies have become a very popular and delicious diet. The blend of fruits and vegetables make it tastier and healthier for everyone. It is advisable to drink the smoothie twice a day to acquire all the required nutrients. It is a great option for the kids!!! Consuming smoothies on regular basis helps in reducing weight and make the overall mechanism of the body more efficient. It also reduces the desire of eating unhealthy food to some extent. It is also surveyed that having a healthy glass of smoothie daily helps in overcoming the chronic diseases. The nutritional content of the smoothie helps in healing the injuries quickly. It also contributes a lot in maintaining the physical and mental well being of the individuals. It is said that when the body is given the natural food contents that they can heal easily.

Green smoothies have become very popular among the individuals for its taste and nutrient content. The effect of smoothies is best if we have them in morning. It keeps the person active and full of energy for the whole day. It is considered to be a good stabilizer for the patients of blood sugar. While making the smoothies the nutritional content should be kept in mind. The fruits and vegetables which are added in the smoothie should be in right amount to retain the dietary value of the smoothie. The fruits and green leafy vegetables which are added in the smoothies contain alkaline which helps in neutralizing the acids in our blood.

We have talked enough about the nutritional benefits of smoothies. There are many health benefits also of smoothies which are discussed in the next chapter of the book.

CHAPTER 4 - HEALTH BENEFITS OF GREEN SMOOTHIES!

What is the best way to have all the nutritional content in your diet? The answer is simple. You need to include lots of green vegetables in your diet. What if you don't like eating green vegetables much? So making a green smoothie is the best way to have all the nutritional contents in our body. The green smoothies help in maintaining the health of our body and protect it from unwanted toxins.

Green smoothies are the complete package of vitamins, minerals, carbohydrates and fiber. The green smoothie consumed on regular basis provides us many health benefits. Some of these benefits are:-

1) Weight loss
    Drinking green smoothies regularly helps us in reducing weight. The fruits and vegetables present in the smoothies help in getting rid from the unwanted toxins present in the body. This gradually leads to weight loss.

2) Easy digestion process
    It is said that the blended fruits and vegetables are easier to digest as compared to raw fruits and vegetables. Smoothies are the best way to assimilate nutrition in our body with smooth digestion mechanism.

3) Presence of Antioxidants
    Green smoothies are the best source of antioxidants for protecting our body from any kind of disease. They act as a defensive measure for the body.

4) Energy booster
    Green smoothies act as the energy boosters for our body. They are a rich source of vitamins, proteins and minerals which stabilize our digestive system and boost our energy.

5) Mental peace and stability in life
    Another very important health benefit of green smoothie is getting mental peace and stability in life. The individuals set a positive mind towards everything. It also helps in reducing anxiety and stress.

6) More intake of fiber

Fiber constitutes as the most vital form for our body. We get fibers in our diet when we drink juices or eat raw vegetables. The best way to have the maximum amount of fiber in our body is to include green smoothies in our diet.

7) Clear and fair skin

Since smoothies are higher in fiber content so it helps in reducing the intoxicants present in our body. This ultimately gives us a fairer and clear skin.

8) Lessen the carvings for junk food

Another very important benefit of green smoothie is that it reduces the cravings for unhealthy food like sweets, sugar etc. Moreover the smoothies are rich is chlorophyll therefore it also rejuvenates our body and reduce the carvings. Thus green smoothie is a good energy drink, which gives lot of health benefits. Read the next chapter to know that how you can reduce weight by drinking green smoothie!!!

CHAPTER 5 - GREEN SMOOTHIES- AN EFFECTIVE WAY TO REDUCE YOUR WEIGHT!

Are you fed up of dietary medicines? Are they not doing any good to you? Do you want to reduce your excessive weight? If answer to all these questions is yes then the very first thing you need to do is to replace the junk food with fresh fruits and green vegetables in your refrigerator. I think by studying the above chapters you have got some idea about the importance of fruits and vegetables in your diet. They are the best source of proteins, vitamins, fibers, carbohydrates and minerals. They keep our immune system strong and heal our injuries quickly. Now how to reduce your weight without getting any kind of weakness? The best answer to this is the t? ?n?lud? green smoothie in your diet. The people who are not able to eat vegetables in solid form can eat it in liquid form by making green smoothies. Drinking green smoothie daily is the best way to reduce your excessive weight and tone up your body.

Now in green smoothie weight loss plan you replace the breakfast with fresh smoothies. In lunch also you can have the green smoothie or a little solid food. The dinner should be comprised of whole grains, fruits and vegetables to maintain a balanced diet. A green smoothie is the cheapest way of reducing body weight. It is not possible for everyone to go for dietary supplements and medicines. They are very expensive. Moreover at times they also cause allergies. So it's better to stick to the natural way of losing your weight. Including green vegetables and fruits in your diet will help in acquiring all the nutrients naturally.

Our body is very delicate. It demands natural things to function properly. The medicines and dietary supplements don't last for long. In fact taking the medicines on regular basis affects our immune system to a great extent. It is always good to stick to natural ways to lose weight. It is advisable that if a person wants to reduce weight then they should blend the fruits and vegetables in an equal proportion. According to some surveys conducted in US, it was estimated that 60% fruits and 40% green vegetables should be mixed to make an effective and delicious smoothie. Now the question has arisen that how to make a delicious smoothie? To know more about it read the next chapter of the book.

CHAPTER 6 - HOW TO PREPARE DELICIOUS RAW GREEN SMOOTHIES?

Raw green smoothie is nothing but a blend of fresh fruits and vegetables. It is taken as a juice which is rich in nutritional values. It provides more energy and strength as compared to fruits and vegetables eaten raw.

Raw green smoothie is very easy to prepare. The most important thing which is required is the correct equipment to blend the fruits and vegetables. If the individuals have just started drinking the green smoothie drink, then they should maintain the fruits and vegetable ratio as 60:40. As they will get used to it they can reverse the ratio and include more of green vegetables in their diet.

Now the next question which arises in our mind is what kind of fruits and vegetables to be used for green smoothie. Usually all types of green vegetables will do, but people prefer more of spinach and lettuce in the starting. It is recommended that the vegetables should be rotated well in the blender. The individuals who have just started with the green smoothie can start with spinach as it doesn't have any specific taste.

About the fruits, we can use any type of fruits in the smoothie. Once the fruits and vegetables are decided they are put into the blender and mixed with water. After mixing them, it is wise to first taste the smoothie and figure out what is missing. If the individuals want it to be sweeter then they can add honey or more ripe fruits to it. If they want it more liquid then they can add water to it. If you want the smoothie to be more energetic then add more green leafy vegetables to it.

It is advisable to drink the smoothies in breakfast. Having a green smoothie is the best substitute for other breakfast items. The individuals can also prefer to have the smoothie during lunch as well. It will help in boosting their energy and will relax their mind. Green smoothies also provide many other benefits like weight loss, quick healing of injuries, acts as sugar stabilizer, cures chronic illness like diabetes, heart diseases, asthma etc. These green smoothies are enriched in nutrients which nourish our body. Drinking green smoothies regularly increases our carving of green vegetables. It reduces our interest towards junk food intake as well. So introducing green smoothies is the best way to have a balanced diet.

CHAPTER 7 - HOW TO MAKE YOUR GREEN SMOOTHIE TASTES GOOD?

Everyone has different taste buds and according to the taste buds people prefer to eat. Some like to eat more of sweets while some prefer spicy. Now talking about green smoothies, there are ways by which we can make it taste good. Green Smoothies is a blend of delicious fruits and vegetables. In the starting it might happen that the person doesn't like the taste of the green smoothie. So it's better to add more of ripe fruits in the beginning than the green vegetables. As the individuals get used to it they can substitute the fruits with more of green leafy vegetables. Besides this there are certain other ways by which we can add flavor to our green smoothie.

- Add peeled 'Lemon' to the green smoothie to make it tangier. Not only this, but by adding lemon to the green smoothie, we can save it to have later.

- 'Ginger' can be added to the green smoothies prepared during winter. It helps in adding warmth to your body.

- Then there is 'Cinnamon' which is used with apples to give the green smoothies a more delicious taste.

- People also prefer to add 'Vanilla' in their smoothies to cut the taste of green leafy vegetables.

- Then there are 'health fats' like butter milk, raw butter and avocado to make the green smoothie tastes good.

- Individuals can also replace the water with 'cream' or 'milk'. It will make the green smoothie more smooth and delicious.

- People can also use 'ice cubes' to make chilled green smoothies.

Not only the above stated ways but you can also experiment with some other ways too. It all depends on your likes and dislikes. As you get use to the green smoothies you can always experiment with other ingredients. Adding flax seeds in the green smoothies will help in providing a rich source of fiber content to the body. Mix the different fruits and vegetables and enjoy the different flavors. It is a very delicious way to increase the nutrient content in our body. Moreover it is very easy to prepare and tastes very delicious. Green smoothies are considered to be the most delicious way of nourishing our body with all the proteins, vitamins, minerals and fibers

CHAPTER 8 - HOW TO INCORPORATE GREEN SMOOTHIES IN OUR DAILY DIET?

Why not choose a healthy drink instead of colas and sodas? Green smoothies are considered to be a healthy way to get rid of all the man-made beverages. All the man-made beverages contain the artificial sweeteners and powders which are not at all effective and healthy. It's good to include fresh fruits and vegetables in your diet. Fruits already contain sweets in them which can be used instead of the artificial sweeteners. The natural sugar content can easily be metabolized by the body.

Now the question which comes in our mind is how we can add the green smoothies in our daily diet? Well!!! We can skip our breakfast with one glass of green smoothie. Though there are no limits. The individuals can take as much smoothie as they want because it is safe and healthy. As discussed earlier also, the normal ratio of fruits and vegetables in green smoothies is 60:40, i.e. 60% of fruits and 40% of vegetables. However, as the individuals get used to it, they can substitute the ratio. The individuals can also have the green smoothies for lunch as well.

Green smoothies are basically recommended for vegetarian people. Green smoothies are very effective for everyone. They help in making a balanced life style. Green smoothies help in providing all the essentials nutrients to our body. It is a perfect diet for everyone. Greens are the most important part of our body. Maximum energy that we get in our body is from the green vegetables that we eat. So, it is very important to include the vegetables in our daily life. It is also said that don't fully depend on the green smoothies. Have a balanced diet with all the other food products also. Green smoothies are just to build your metabolism and keep you fit and healthy. Now-a-days people are substituting it with breakfast and lunch. It is healthy but they shouldn't forget about the other nutrition providing dishes. You can have the green smoothie any time you want. However, make sure that it is freshly prepared with all different fruits and vegetables. Raw foods are the most healthy food items. Instead of having it in solid form, blend it and have it in the liquid form. This will give more energy and nutrients to our body than the solid ones. Experiment with the different fruits and vegetables to change the taste of the green smoothies.

CHAPTER 9 – 25 QUICK AND EASY RECIPES FOR WEIGHT LOSS

1 GREEN'S SMOOTHIE

Servings: 2

Ingredients:
1 c. kale or collard greens (packed stems removed & coarsely chopped)
1 apple (coarsely chopped)
1 ripe banana
1/2 c. fresh flat-leaf parsley leaves
2¼ c. water

Directions:
1. Take a blender; add & combine all the ingredients.
2. Blend them well until smooth.
3. If the mixture is too thick, then add in a little more water.

2 CITRUS GREEN SMOOTHIE

Servings: 4

Ingredients:
4-5 ice cubes
2 oranges juice
1/2 lemon juice
1 c. spinach
1 c. kale
1 banana
1 handful fresh mint & coriander

Directions:
1. Add the ice cubes into the blender.
2. Add in the orange & lemon juice.
3. Then, add the spinach, kale, banana, mint & coriander into the blender.
4. Blend until smooth

3 CUCUMBER CELERY LIME

Servings: 2

Ingredients:
1/2 c. ice
4 stalks celery heart (chopped into large chunks)
1 small cucumber (peeled, chopped & seeds removed)
1/2 lime juice
1/2 c. water

Directions:
1. Add the ice cubes into the blender.
2. Add in the water, then celery heart, cucumber and lime juice into the blender.
3. Blend until smooth.

4 SALAD SMOOTHIE

Servings: 2

Ingredients:
4-5 ice cubes
1 c. greens (arugula, spinach & salad mix, etc.)
1 carrot
1 sweet pepper
1/2 tomato
1/2 avocado
1/2 c. pine nuts (soaked)
1 garlic
Dill or parsley
1/2 grapefruit juice

Directions:
1. Add the ice cubes into the blender.
2. Then, add all the remaining ingredients into the blender.
3. Blend until smooth.

5 PAPAYA APPLE GREEN SMOOTHIE

Servings: 1

Ingredients:
2-4 ice cubes
1 c. papaya
1/2 c. kale
1/2 c. spinach
1/2 banana
1/2 green apple

Directions:
1. Add the ice cubes into the blender.
2. Then, add all the remaining ingredients into the blender.
3. Blend until smooth.

6 CUCUMBER LEMON GREEN SMOOTHIE

Servings: 4

Ingredients:
1 handful of ice
1 c. water
1 lemon juice
Fresh ginger (sliced & peeled)
1/2 cucumber (peeled)
1 handful fresh parsley
2 handfuls spinach
2 sticks kale (stems remove)
1/2 green banana

Directions:
1. Add the ice cubes into the blender.
2. Then, add all the remaining ingredients into the blender.
3. Blend until smooth.

7 GREEN TEA GREEN SMOOTHIE

Servings: 4

Ingredients:
8-10 ice cubes
1 avocado (peeled & seeded)
1 organic apple (cored & unpeeled)
1 frozen banana
1 c. baby spinach (loosely packed)
1 c. kale (loosely packed & stems removed)
1 c. green tea (unsweetened)

Directions:
1. Add the ice cubes into the blender.
2. Then, add all the remaining ingredients into the blender.
3. Blend until smooth. You can add less green tea for thicker smoothie.

8 GREEN DETOX SMOOTHIE

Servings: 2

Ingredients:
4-5 ice cubes
1 cup water
2 celery stalks (chopped)
1 small cucumber (chopped)
2 kale leaves
1 handful spinach
1 handful fresh parsley or cilantro
1 lemon (peeled)
1 apple (seeded, cored & chopped)

Directions:
1. Add the ice cubes into the blender.
2. Add in the water and then, all the remaining ingredients into the blender.
3. Blend until smooth. You can add less green tea for thicker smoothie.

9 ORANGE & BERRY SMOOTHIE

Servings: 2

Ingredients:
2 oranges (peeled, pith removed & sliced into chunks)
1 c. frozen blueberries
1 c. frozen raspberries

Directions:
1. Take a blender; add & combine all the ingredients.
2. Blend them well until smooth.

10 MINT & CHOCOLATE CHIP GREEN SMOOTHIE

Servings: 1

Ingredients:
3/4 c. water
1 tsp. almond butter
1 frozen banana
1/4 – 1/3 cup fresh mint leaves
1 large handful of spinach
1/2 tsp. vanilla
1 tsp. raw honey (or your favorite sweetener)
1/2 tbsp. cacao nibs
Optional ingredients
1 tsp. cacao powder (for extra chocolaty taste)
1 scoop of your favorite protein powder
Directions:
1. Take a blender; add & combine all the ingredients except cacao nibs.
2. Blend them well until smooth.
3. Then, add in the cacao nibs & pulse for a few seconds until you have chunks.
4. Next, garnished with fresh mint & cacao nibs on top.
5. Serve it immediately

11 COCONUT MANGO SPINACH SMOOTHIE

Servings: 1

Ingredients:
1 c. frozen coconut milk (cubes)
1 c. mango (fresh cut & frozen)
1½ c. filtered water
1½ c. (0.8 oz.) fresh organic spinach
2 tbsp. maple syrup or few drops of stevia or honey
1 tbsp. hemp protein powder

Directions:
1. Firstly freeze the mangoes for at least 2 hours.
2. Then, in a blender; add & combine all the ingredients.
2. Blend them well until well incorporated.

12 CARROT & GINGER SMOOTHIE

Servings: 2

Ingredients:
1 bunch of carrots with some greens
1 avocado
1/2 lemon
About 1/3" fresh ginger
Pinch of sea salt
Pinch of cayenne pepper
Spring or distilled water (as required)

Directions:
1. In a blender or juicer; add & combine all the ingredients.
2. Add in the clean water to cover all the ingredients.
3. Blend them well until well incorporated. & serve immediately.

13 SPINACH & ORANGE SMOOTHIE

Servings: 1

Ingredients:
Package of spinach
½ cup of orange juice

Directions:
1. In a blender; mix fresh green leaves of spinach with orange juice.
2. Blend them well until smooth.
3. Next, pour it into a big mug & add couple of ice cubes to chill.

14 SPINACH, PARSLEY & APPLE SMOOTHIE

Servings: 4

Ingredients:
1 tsp. ginger root
1 bunch parsley
1/2 lemon (juiced)
2 apples (cored)
1 c. spinach
1 medium cucumber
3 celery sticks

Directions:
1. In a blender; add & combine all the ingredients.
2. Blend them well on high speed for about 1 minute or until smooth.

15 LETTUCE & FRUITY GREEN SMOOTHIE

Servings: 4

Ingredients:
1 head of organic romaine lettuce
1½ c. water
4 stalks of fresh celery
1 apple
1 banana
1 cored pear
½ c. fresh lemon juice
¼ bunch of cilantro (optional)
¼ bunch of fresh parsley (optional)

Directions:
1. In a blender; add in the lettuce & water & blend well on low until smooth.
2. Then, add in the celery, apple & pear; blend them on medium speed.
3. Next, add in the cilantro & parsley; blend on same speed.
4. Now, add in the banana & lemon; blend on high for about 1 minute or until smooth.
5. Finally, pour it into the serving cups & decorate with lemon slices.

16 KALE & APPLE SMOOTHIE

Servings: 1

Ingredients:
3/4 c. chopped kale (ribs & thick stems removed)
1 small stalk of celery (chopped)
1/2 banana
1/2 c. apple juice
1/2 c. ice
1 tbsp. fresh lemon juice

Directions:
1. In a blender; add & combine all the ingredients.
2. Blend them well until smooth & frothy.

17 KIWI GREEN SMOOTHIE

Servings: 1

Ingredients:
1 c. kale leaves (chopped)
1 c. Romaine lettuce (chopped)
1 c. Swiss chard leaves (chopped)
½ c. ripe bananas (sliced)
½ kiwi fruit
1/2 lemon (juiced)
1 c. distilled water
1 tsp. bee pollen
½ tsp. maca powder

Directions:
1. In a blender; add & combine all the ingredients.
2. Blend them well until smooth.
3. You can use mango or papaya as substitute of kiwis (if out of season).

18 COCONUT PINEAPPLE & SPINACH SMOOTHIE

Servings: 2

Ingredients:
1 c. water
4 c. pineapple (chopped)
½ c. coconut (shredded)
1 c. spinach or other mild greens

Directions:
1. In a blender; add & blend the dry ingredients with water for a short time.
2. Then, blend the greens (if using)
3. Next, blend the fruit & the rest of the ingredients until smooth.

19 LOW CARB GREEN SMOOTHIE

Servings: 2

Ingredients:
1 c. coconut water
1 tbsp. almond butter
1/4 c. wheat grass
2 c. spinach
1 scoop low carb chocolate protein
1" slice of banana
Pinch of stevia (optional)
1/2 c. ice

Directions:
1. In a blender; add & combine all the ingredients.
2. Then, blend for about 1 minute or until smooth.

20 GREEN POWER SMOOTHIE

Servings: 2

Ingredients:
2-3 bananas
1 c. rice or nut milk
1 spoonful raw almond butter
1 scoop raw hemp protein
1 scoop raw cacao powder
Sprinkle of spirulina
Handful of wheat grass (sliced & rinse)
1-2 c. spinach leaves
2-3 large kale leaves
1 scoop of ice (optional)

Directions:
1. In a blender; add & combine all the ingredients.
2. Blend them well until smooth.

21 PUMPKIN, HAZELNUT & COCONUT GREEN SMOOTHIE

Servings: 1

Ingredients:
1/2 c. pumpkin puree
1 banana (peeled)
10 raw hazelnuts (soaked for about 4 hours)
1 scoop pumpkin seed protein powder
1/2 tsp. cinnamon
Dash of nutmeg
2 c. fresh baby spinach
8-10 oz. of coconut water

Directions:
1. Take a blender; add in the liquid with the soft fruit.
2. Then, add in the greens.
2. Blend them well for about 30 seconds or until smooth & creamy.

22 LUSTROUS GREEN SMOOTHIE

Servings: 1

Ingredients:
1-2 bananas
½ c. frozen peaches
½ c. frozen mango
2 handfuls of spinach
Water (as required)

Directions:
1. Take a blender; add in all the ingredients.
2. Blend them well until smooth.

23 PINEAPPLE & MINT SMOOTHIE

Servings: 2

Ingredients:
1 c. water
2 c. pineapple (fresh or frozen)
1 avocado
1 c. mint leaves
1 c. spinach leaves or other mild green

Directions:
1. Take a blender; add & combine all the ingredients.
2. Blend them well until smooth.

24 BLUEBERRY & PINEAPPLE SMOOTHIE

Servings: 2

Ingredients:
1 c. pineapple
2 tomatoes
1 c. blueberries (frozen or fresh)
¼ c. coriander
1 c. spinach leaves or other mild leafy green
1 celery stick (chopped)
1 squeeze of lemon (to taste)
Ice (as required)

Directions:
1. Take a blender; add & combine all the ingredients.
2. Blend them well until smooth.

25 CLASSIC PEAR SMOOTHIE

Servings: 1

Ingredients:
1 ½ - 2 pears (regular size, no stalk & chopped)
1 c. water
2 c. strong greens (or 1 cup mild & 1 cup strong)
2 tbsp. lemon or lime juice
Ice (as required)

Directions:
1. Take a blender; add & combine all the ingredients.
2. Blend them well until smooth.

CONCLUSION

To conclude about Green Smoothies we can say that it is the most promising health drink ever. Individuals who eat less of green vegetables should include the green smoothies in their daily diet to cover all the nutrients which they are deficient off. Green smoothies are a rich source of vitamins, minerals, fibers and proteins. It is very helpful in reducing excessive weight and overcoming chronic illness like diabetes, heart disease, asthma etc. Green Smoothies can be prepared in seconds. It can be called as fast food by nature.

People have started adding this in their daily diet. They are even inculcating this habit in their children. It is suggested to consume the green smoothie immediately after making it. This is because if we keep the smoothie for long time then all its nutrients will be lost. It is considered to be the best way for the people who are not able to eat the raw vegetables. By mixing the green vegetables with fruits they can easily drink it. Moreover it is very easy to digest. According to a survey it is shown that chewing leads to forty percent of the absorption of food while blending leads to ninety percent of the digestion. So it is very clear that drinking a glass of smoothie is far better than having a bowl of salad daily.

Finally, if you enjoyed this book, please take the time to share your thoughts and post a review on Amazon. It'd be greatly appreciated!
Thank you and good luck!

ABOUT THE AUTHOR

Russell Warrens's passion with nutrition lead his to a career in cooking and healthcare. Along with being a healthy cooking coach, he has also a published author.

He writes on topics close to her heart - cooking, green smoothie, weight loss and living healthy. When he's not busy writing health guides and recipe books, he enjoys cooking for family and friends, reading and exploring new tastes, ideas and places.

His ultimate goal is to educate as many people as possible about the healthy live , healing powers of food and how to easily incorporate these changes into daily life.

Made in the USA
Las Vegas, NV
23 January 2022

42173667R00029